INCREASE YOUR WORD POWER

2

Woxbrandt / Kunze

BEAVER BOOKS

© **Beaver Books**   Dr. C. Kunze / B. Woxbrandt

Alle Rechte vorbehalten

All rights reserved. No part of this publication may be reproduced or utilized, in any forms or by any means, without the prior permission of the copyright holders and publishers.

Die Deutsche Bibliothek - CIP-Einheitsaufnahme

Woxbrandt, Barbro:
Increase your wordpower / Woxbrandt / Kunze. - Frankfurt am Main : Beaver Books

2 (1997)
    ISBN 3 - 926686 - 24 - 3

BEAVER BOOKS, Marburger Str. 15, 60487 Frankfurt/Main
Tel. 069/774047 • Fax 069/704635

INCREASE YOUR WORDPOWER · 2

How Do you Do?	**Everyday English**	5
When the Cat's away	**Proverbs**	6
Confusable Verbs	**Confusables**	8
Keep your Fingers Crossed	**Idioms and Adjectives**	10
Wordpower Rockets	**Word Game**	12
In a Class of its Own	**Classifications (Hypernyms)**	13
Time for a Rhyme	**Pronunciation**	14
Super-duper razzmatazz	**Pronunciation / Word-formation**	15
Star Signs	**Adjectives describing People**	16
Compose a Compound	**Word-formation: Compounds**	18
Word Pyramids	**Word Game**	19
Synonym Quartets	**Synonyms**	20
Hair-raising Synonyms	**Synonyms / Word-formation**	21
Of Compounds	**Word-Formation**	22
Looking Good	**Phrasal Verbs**	23
Homographs	**Homographs**	24
Homophones	**Pronunciation**	25
For better for worse	**Antonyms**	26
Double Antonyms	**Antonyms**	27
Making Headlines	**Newspaper English**	28
Confusable Adjectives	**Confusables**	30
Made in America	**American English**	32
What's Cooking?	**American Idioms**	33
Now you're Talking	**English in Everyday Situations**	34
Mixed Bag Quiz	**General Vocabulary Quiz**	36
Look for Links	**'Day is to sun as night is to moon'**	37
Look in the right Place	**Semantic Field**	38
Famous Landmarks	**Semantic Field**	39
Know the Ins and Outs	**Phrasal Verbs**	40
Get your Teeth into English	**Colloquial English**	41
Just like a Bull in a China Shop	**Idioms of Comparison**	42
Fixed Phrases	**Word-Formation**	44
Up or Down?	**Phrasal Verbs**	45
All's Well that Ends Well	**Word-formation: Compounds**	46
Ladies & Gentlemen	**Word-Formation: Binomials**	47
Add your Ad	**The Language of Advertising**	48
Who is Who?	**Semantic Field: People**	50
Gerund Compounds	**Word-Formation**	51
American & British English	**American English**	52
Confusable Nouns	**Confusables**	54
Be as good as your Word	**General Vocabulary Quiz**	56
The Golden Middle	**Word-formation**	57
Professional Compounds	**Semantic Field: Jobs & Professions**	58
When all is said and done	**Idioms with 'all'**	59
Quantities	**Partitives**	60
Scrabble	**Word Game**	61
Fixed Phrases	**Word-Formation**	62
Dial A word	**Word Game**	63

INCREASE YOUR WORDPOWER

EVERYDAY ENGLISH

How do you do? • Fixed Replies 5
Now you're Talking! • Everyday Situations 34
Get your Teeth into Colloquial English 41

SEMANTIC FIELDS

In a Class of its own • Hyperonyms 13
Look in the right Place 38
Famous Landmarks 39
Who is Who? – People 50
Professional Compounds – Jobs & Professions 58

WORD GAMES

Wordpower Rockets 12
Word Pyramids 19
Scrabble 61
Dial a Word 63

WORD-FORMATION

Super-duper razzmatazz 15
Compose a Compound 18
Of Compounds 22
Fixed Phrases 44
All's well that Ends well 46
Ladies & Gentlemen • Binomials 47
Gerund Compounds 51
The Golden Middle 57
Quantities • Partitives 60
Fixed Phrases 62

PHRASAL VERBS

Looking Good 23
Knowing the Ins and Outs 40
Up or Down? 45

PRONUNCIATION

Time for a Rhyme 14
Homophones 25

IDIOMS & PROVERBS

When the Cat's away 6
Keep your Fingers Crossed 10
Body Language 11
Just like a Bull in a China Shop 42
Idioms of Comparison 43
When all is said and done 59

SYNONYMS & ANTONYMS

Synonyms & Synonym Quartets 20
Hair-raising Synonyms 21
For better for worse 26
Double Antonyms 27

CONFUSABLES

Confusable Verbs 8
Confusable Adjectives 30
Confusable Nouns 54

MISCELLANEOUS

Star Signs 16
Homographs 24
Making Headlines • Newspaper English 28
Made in America • American English 32
What's Cooking? • American Idioms 33
Mixed Bag Quiz 36
Look for Links 37
The Language of Advertising 48
American & British English 52
Be as good as your Word 56

How do you do?

It has been said that the definition of an Englishman is someone who says 'sorry' if somebody else steps on his foot. Whether this is true or not, the fact is that in certain situations English-speaking people expect certain types of reply to a particular question, statement or occurrence. If you meet someone for the first time, for instance, and he or she says 'How do you do?' you reply 'How do you do?'. You could almost say that such replies are part of a ritual; you would sound odd, if you left them out or said something else.

Take the replies from the grey box and put them next to the appropriate sentence.

Congratulations.	Neither can I.	Pleased to meet you. I'm John.
Good luck!	Not at all.	Thanks. The same to you.
I certainly hope so.	Oh, I'm sorry.	That's very kind of you, thank you.
I'm fine, thanks, and you?	Oh, never mind.	Yes, please. / No, thank you.

1. Thank you for all your help. _____

2. I won £ 800 in the National Lottery last Saturday. _____

3. I can't stand greasy food. _____

4. Do you think this rain will stop soon? _____

5. I'm sorry about having lost your pen. _____

6. Have a nice weekend. _____

7. Hello, how are you? _____

8. I'm sitting my final exam tomorrow. _____

9. Excuse me, but you are standing on my foot. _____

10. Can I help you with this suitcase? _____

11. Have you met my old friend Mark? _____

12. Would you like a cup of tea? _____

WHEN THE CAT'S AWAY...
...the mice will play

Something went wrong with these proverbs. Pair them up correctly!

1. As you sow _____ think alike.

2. A stitch in time _____ might fly!

3. You win some _____ nothing gained.

4. He who laughs last _____ crying over spilt milk.

5. One good turn _____ sweeps clean.

6. Live _____ so you reap.

7. Great minds _____ speak louder than words.

8. A new broom _____ saves nine.

9. Beggars _____ are soon parted.

10. Pigs _____ can't be choosers.

11. It's no use _____ you lose some.

12. Nothing ventured _____ deserves another.

13. Actions _____ and let live.

14. A fool and his money _____ laughs longest.

... AND *P*IGS MIGHT FLY!

Pigs might fly
Live and let live
Look before you leap
Every dog has its day
It never rains but it pours
Beggars can't be choosers
It's no use crying over spilt milk
Never judge a book by its cover
Where there's a will, there's a way
When the cat's away, the mice will play

Look at these proverbs which express in a few words a truth relating to everyday experience. Can you complete the dialogues or sentences below by adding the appropriate proverbs?

1. My chances of winning the jackpot in that lottery are very small, but you never know . . .

2. 'Are you really going to take that awful job', he said. She replied 'It's not that bad and besides . . .'.

3. I'm sure your chance will come soon. After all, . . .

4. Don't be too hard on your son, after all you were young once; so . . .

5. Our new neighbour seemed very snobbish and arrogant at first, but actually he's very friendly. As they say, . . .

6. Don't buy the first second-hand car you're offered just because it's cheap; my advice is . . .

7. On our holiday the car broke down, our money was stolen, and the children fell ill. You know what they say:

8. We should have bought a bigger house a year ago when the prices were low! However, . . .

9. My nephew is determined to be a millionaire by the age of twenty-five. Who knows, . . .

10. As soon as his parents had gone out, his friends starting coming and they had a wild party. It's always the same:

CONFUSABLE VERBS

**The following verbs are often confused.
Write the correct word in the sentences below. Watch your tenses!**

| lay | borrow | bring | hear | do | go up | say | see |
| lie | lend | take | listen | make | get up | tell | watch |

1. What did your wife _____ when you _____ her about the accident?
2. Could you _____ a birthday cake for Christine?
3. I will _____ you two pounds, if you give me the money back tomorrow.
4. Tom _____ Janet to the cinema last night.
5. Don't _____ in bed all morning. Get up!
6. I wouldn't _____ no to a glass of beer or two.
7. I told her four times what to do, but she wasn't _____ !
8. Why don't you sit down? I'll _____ you a nice cup of tea.
9. The neighbour's cat has been _____ our budgie all morning.
10. We can _____ in the elevator if you have difficulties managing the stairs.
11. May I _____ your English dictionary, please?
12. When you come here tomorrow, please _____ your books.
13. He _____ carefully, but couldn't _____ everything.
14. He _____ his coat on the chair and took the paper which was _____ there.
15. I usually _____ at 8.30 in the morning.
16. She _____ us she would go home.
17. He _____ his best, but he still _____ many mistakes.
18. Please _____ this letter to the Post Office and _____ me some stamps back.
19. I have never _____ a bird like that before!
20. How many eggs does this hen _____ each week?
21. Sorry, Mum, I didn't have time to _____ the beds this morning.
22. He stood there _____ the crowd, when he _____ his wife coming round the corner.

*C*hoose the correct word in each of the following sentences and then use the empty line to write your own sentence containing the alternative word to show you've understood the difference in meaning.

1. I'm late, I shall have to *drive / go* by taxi.

2. At what age do babies learn to *go / walk*?

3. He has managed to *save / spare* enough to buy a mountain bike.

4. Who *discovered / invented* the telephone?

5. Mr Briton *carries / bears* an umbrella wherever he goes, whether it's raining or not.

6. Would you *draw / pull* the curtains, please!

7. I think I *forgot / left* my handbag behind at the theatre last night.

8. Could you *remember / remind* me to phone the doctor this afternoon to make an appointment for my mother?

9. The jacket doesn't fit properly. I shall have to have it *changed / altered* before going on holiday.

10. I like you in that colour, it really *fits / suits* you. You should wear it more often!

11. We saw Karajan *conducting / directing* the Berlin Symphony Orchestra in New York many years ago.

12. Didn't you *notice / remark* what she was wearing? A see-through blouse!

13. Are you going to *pass / spend* a long time in the States?

14. Who *learnt / taught* you to play the piano so well, John?

KEEP YOUR FINGERS CROSSED

with English Idioms

'To keep one's fingers crossed' is an **idiom** or **idiomatic expression**: There are many informal expressions in English containing words referring to parts of the body. The way in which idiomatic expressions are put together is often odd and illogical, but everybody understands them.

*W*e'll keep our fingers crossed for you

- We'll hope for a good result and good luck
- We think you are about to do something foolish
- We think you are going to hurt your fingers

*J*ohn didn't have a leg to stand on

- John had broken both legs in an accident
- John had no excuse for his actions or views
- John had to go down on his knees to ask for forgiveness

*T*he thief took to his heels when he saw the policeman

- The thief quickly put his shoes on
- The thief ran away when he saw the policeman coming
- The thief quickly sat down on his heels to hide

*G*eorge waited on his wife hand and foot

- George never did anything on his own
- He sat at his wife's feet all day and held her hand
- He did everything his wife wanted

*I*f you poke your nose into something, you

- smell a cake to see if it's cooked
- interfere with something even though it doesn't concern you
- consider someone less important than yourself

*M*y ears are burning!

- The sun is very hot today and I think my ears got sunburnt
- Someone must be talking about me
- This music is too loud for me; my ears are hot and hurting

*M*ark and Tom are always at loggerheads with each other

- They always do everything together
- They always disagree very strongly with each other
- They can never agree whose haircut is the best

*R*ussell has a sweet tooth

- He has one gold filling and likes to show it
- He likes to eat sweet things
- He has a sweet smile

*M*elanie is the apple of her mother's eye

- Mum is very fond of or proud of Melanie
- Mum thinks Melanie should eat more apples
- Mum thinks Melanie's eyes are green like apples

Body Language

Look at the definitions in the grey box. Then use these definitions to rewrite the sentences below in a less colloquial way. Make changes where necessary.

> to be ill in bed
> to feel sure about something
> to watch or look after somebody or something
> to say what another person was about to say
> to remain serious
> to be very busy
>
> to meet and talk to people, especially famous people
> to be involved in everything that happens
> to try very hard to think of something
> to look or feel unhappy and miserable
> to be kind and considerate to other people
> to be willing to do almost anything to get something

1. Peter caught pneumonia and *was on his back* for several weeks.

2. I can *feel it in my bones* that Anne is the right girl for me.

3. I'll *keep an eye on* the baby while you're out shopping.

4. Oh definitely, I agree with you. In fact you *took the words out of my mouth*.

5. James is terribly vain. He likes to *rub shoulders with* the rich and famous.

6. Mr Nosey-Parker likes to *have a finger in every pie*.

7. The headmaster's voice sounded so silly that it was difficult for us to *keep a straight face*.

8. We shall *have our hands full* when our visitors arrive from Norway.

9. What's wrong? You look *down in the mouth* today.

10. Susie is a bit dominant but she *has her heart in the right place*.

11. I was *racking my brains* to find something to talk about.

12. She would *give her right arm* for a job in the Civil Service.

WORDPOWER ROCKETS

Form words with the letters from the rocket. You can use each letter as many times as you wish.
3 Letters = 1 Point; 4 Letters = 2 Points; 5 Letters = 3 Points; 6 Letters = 4 Points; More = 5 Points; All: 12 Points

3 Letters _____

4 Letters _____

5 Letters _____

6 Letters _____

More _____

All Letters

K

3 Letters _____

4 Letters _____

5 Letters _____

6 Letters _____

More _____

All Letters

O

POINTS: **10** Take-off • **20** Try more boosters • **30** Gaining height • **40** In Orbit • **50** Stratosphere • **60** Planet Genius!

IN A CLASS OF ITS OWN!

Example: Rose, tulip, iris = *Flowers*

Letters in the fat squares down = **the most famous English-speaking playwright** ▼

Breakfast, lunch, dinner	=
Eel, shark, herring	=
Wheat, barley, rye	=
Tea, whiskey, mineral water	=
Knives, forks, spoons	=
Bible, travel guide, dictionary	=
Rome, London, Washington	=
Dollar, yen, rouble	=
Iron, copper, silver	=
Truly, beautifully, sadly	=
Susan, Timothy, Charles	=

Letters in the fat squares down = **you may have it on your birthday** ▼

General, major, lieutenant	=
Love, hate, fear	=
Ring, necklace, brooch	=
Cholera, malaria, cancer	=
One, eight, twenty-nine	=
Kitchen, attic, study	=
British, French, American	=
Asia, Europe, Africa	=
Christianity, Buddhism, Islam	=
Basketball, tennis, hockey	=
Tango, waltz, rumba	=

TIME FOR A RHYME

Each word in the grey box rhymes with one of the words below; pair them up correctly.

blue	bread	break	bruise	bud	eight	flour	give	heart	height
hum	laid	lurk	ocean	puff	roar	sane	shriek	stone	word

ache _____   cart _____   motion _____   said _____

bird _____   come _____   plate _____   shoe _____

blood _____   leak _____   power _____   sieve _____

blues _____   light _____   rain _____   thrown _____

bore _____   made _____   rough _____   work _____

ODD ONE OUT

Of the four words in the following lines three rhyme and one is the 'odd one out'.

bone	own	(shone)	groan		power	lower	our	flour
course	horse	worse	force		site	eight	height	right
hair	care	pear	pier		heard	bird	word	sword
toast	most	cost	roast		dear	swear	deer	mere
bowl	howl	soul	coal		north	worth	birth	earth
dumb	come	hum	home		weak	freak	meek	break
mown	loan	clown	lone		knew	new	now	due
no	grow	mow	now		come	home	comb	foam
raw	pour	pure	saw		town	alone	shown	flown

You must excuse Harry, he's in that awkward phase between fuddy and duddy

WISHY-WASHY ARGY-BARGY *OR* SUPER-DUPER RAZZMATAZZ?

Fuddy-duddy doesn't mean that Harry is a bit fuddy and also a bit duddy (neither word exists in English). **Fuddy-duddy** is one of many English words, which duplicate a sound or syllable and, by doing so, somehow become more memorable because rhyme appeals powerfully to the human ear. Some of the words below cannot even be found in a dictionary, but people still understand them by association because their sounds suggest a certain meaning or because they echo existing words. You may never have seen the following expressions, but we are confident that you'll be able to pick their correct meaning from the given alternatives.

airy-fairy	○ cool, clever, intellectual	○ cruel and hard	○ vague, impractical, unrealistic
bric-a-brac	○ expensive jewellery	○ cruel and hard	○ small objects of little value
chock-a-block	○ full of cars, people or things	○ punctual	○ empty, deserted, easy to move in
creepy-crawlies	○ insects	○ loud people	○ animals seen on a safari
fiddle-faddle	○ act in a clear, orderly way	○ to impress people	○ waste time in a muddled way
helter-skelter	○ loving and caring	○ hurried and disorganised	○ quiet and peaceful
hocus-pocus	○ unimportant	○ wonderful and valuable	○ confusing and deceiving
hodge-podge	○ an orderly list	○ a disorganised mixture	○ an architect's drawing
hurly-burly	○ peace and quiet	○ noise and activity	○ sadness
mumbo-jumbo	○ a scientific discussion	○ meaningless ritual, nonsense	○ a quarrel between friends
nitty-gritty	○ holiday activities	○ work that is fun	○ basic and important details
namby-pamby	○ strong and active	○ intellectual and artistic	○ feeble, sentimental, weak
palsy-walsy	○ very friendly with each other	○ aggressive	○ boring and stupid
roly-poly	○ long and thin	○ pleasantly round and fat	○ intelligent
razzle-dazzle	○ noisy and showy	○ quick-thinking	○ modest and quiet
super-duper	○ very good	○ tricky, deceptive	○ cheap but worthless
teeny-weeny	○ like a teenager	○ big and burly	○ very small
wishy-washy	○ bursting with energy	○ clean	○ indecisive, vague, half-hearted

ARIES • 21 MAR - 20 APR

Ariens are full of energy – once they've started nobody can stop them, they help everybody. They like to have their own way, but they are generous to their friends and very family-minded. Ariens like to have power and tell other people what to do.

TAURUS • 21 APRIL - 20 MAY

A Taurean always says what he thinks - even if it gets him or her into trouble. Taureans are hard-working and reliable, but they can also be very stubborn. They love food and a good life. People often think that they are a bit slow, but they have a lively brain.

GEMINI • 21 MAY - 20 JUNE

Gemini are always on the move. They love fun, jokes, parties and hate being alone. Gemini learn quickly, but only if something interests them, and they often do not take their work seriously enough. They easily make friends, but also get bored quickly.

CANCER • 21 JUNE - 23 JULY

Cancerians are very sensitive and get hurt easily. They are popular with friends but don't often show their feelings and try to hide their shyness by talking a lot. Family and friends are very important to them. They don't like conflict and like to feel safe.

LEO • 24 JULY - 23 AUGUST

Leos have strong wills and personalities. They are generous and kind, but can also be arrogant: having such a high opinion of themselves, they don't listen to others. Leos are born leaders, when they believe in something they fight for it. They can be very funny.

VIRGO • 24 AUG - 23 SEP

Virgos love order and can be over-pedantic! They are quiet and sometimes too critical of others. However, Virgos are very good organisers, very kind and friendly and would do anything to help their friends - and have a great sense of humour as well!

LIBRA • 24 SEP - 23 OCT

Librans are charming people who hate being alone and try to please everybody. But their popularity can go to their head and make them think they are very important. Their leisure time is often more important to them than work. This can make them unreliable.

SCORPIO • 24 OCT - 22 NOV

Scorpios are active and loyal people. They love practical work like digging the garden. Scorpios have a strong will and always finish what they start. This can cause problems, because they think that they always know best and don't listen to other people.

SAGITTARIUS • 23 NOV - 21 DEC

Sagittarians are always optimistic and open to new ideas and experiments. But when they don't succeed at one thing they just stop and go on to the next. Their big problem is that they have no patience, but they are generous and warm-hearted people.

CAPRICORN • 22 DEC - 20 JAN

Capricorns are hard-working and serious people. Their job and studies are the most important things in their lives. You can totally rely on a Capricorn, but they often are too direct and hurt their friends' feelings. They can also be selfish, and penny-pinching.

AQUARIUS • 21 JAN - 19 FEB

Aquarians are full of great plans and ideals, hate rules and take it easy. Aquarians are open and honest people, but often lose touch with reality and become dreamers. They can be slow to change and like to do things their way. They can also be moody.

PISCES • 20 FEB - 20 MAR

Pisceans are romantic but can be impractical. It is easy to hurt them, even if you try to be nice. They often ask friends what to do, instead of making their own decisions. They have all this imagination and talent, but sometimes don't know what to do with it.

STAR CHARACTERS

1. Read the texts and make a list of the adjectives (friendly, generous, etc.) and phrases (likes to have power, hates being lonely, etc) which describe people.

   Adjectives: _____   **Phrases:** _____

2. Think of people (real or imaginary) who fit these descriptions; describe their behaviour in typical situations.
3. Read the text for your sign. Do you think it is a correct description of your personality?
4. Write a character description of your star sign which you think is correct.

COMPOSE A COMPOUND

*C*ompounds are words that are made up of two words to express a new meaning: a blackboard, for example, is not just a black board (notice also the change in intonation), but is a new and independent word. There are solid compounds, in which the formative words melt into one (blackboard, teapot), and open compounds (coffee cup, dining room); alternatively some compounds can also be spelled with a hyphen (daydream / day-dream; rock garden / rock-garden).

PAIR UP THE ITEMS BELOW TO FORM COMPOUNDS.

SOLID COMPOUNDS ◆ **OPEN COMPOUNDS**

milk		shirt	master		book
sun		box	oil		hour
rain		brush	opinion		star
paper		cloth	package		station
earth		line	picture		car
handle		mind	spark		kitchen
straw		plough	lunch		rate
rail		bird	safety		limit
seat		bar	tennis		poll
sweat		shine	birth		plug
song		belt	police		holiday
tooth		shake	speed		pin
guide		berry	sports		plate
letter		drop	soup		plan
table		way	pop		plant
snow		worm	pot		tanker
master		weight	number		match

WORD PYRAMIDS

Each word in the pyramid is formed by adding a letter to the previous word; rearrange the letters if necessary.

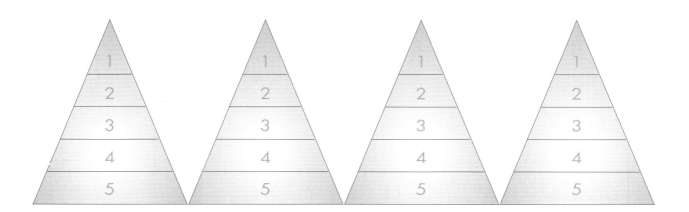

1 First person singular	Short for 'penny'	Indefinite article	Fifth letter of the alphabet
2 Pronoun	A name for a father	Preposition	You and I
3 Healthy	Small, round, green	You do it with food	Opposite of dry
4 An angry hand	Sweet and juicy fruit	Extreme warmth	South, north, east and . .
5 Before all others	Found in an oyster	A cereal	Use too much of something

1 Indefinite article	1 Sounds like an insect	1 Best result in test
2 Preposition	2 To – or not to –	2 Indefinite article
3 Past tense of 'eat'	3 Risk money on a result	3 Hurried
4 Water from the eye	4 Better than better	4 Water from the sky
5 A large box for bottles	5 An animal	5 Means of transport
6 Bring into being	6 Part of the body	6 Stress

SYNONYMS

**Synonyms are words that mean the same or nearly the same as another.
Find the twelve pairs of synonyms in the verb list below. Then write sentences with each pair.**

admire	aid	alter	answer	beat	begin	build	cease
change	comprehend	construct	deceive	defeat	detect	find out	finish
help	respect	respond	scream	shout	start	swindle	understand

1. _____
2. _____
3. _____
4. _____
5. _____
6. _____
7. _____
8. _____
9. _____
10. _____
11. _____
12. _____

SYNONYM QUARTETS

Pair up the synonyms in the grey box with their partners below; then write one sentence with each of them.

| beautiful | clever | correct | daring | dishonest | **dull** | evil | frank |
| frightened | gentle | gloomy | happy | lively | proud | strange | wealthy |

1. slow, sluggish, inactive ___**dull**___
2. affluent, rich, prosperous _____
3. vain, arrogant, conceited _____
4. afraid, fearful, worried _____
5. energetic, active, busy _____
6. alien, exotic, foreign _____
7. candid, open, honest _____
8. tricky, deceitful, lying _____
9. dark, dim, shadowy _____
10. bad, immoral, corrupt _____
11. lovely, pretty, handsome _____
12. brave, courageous, fearless _____
13. right, appropriate, fitting _____
14. calm, cool, peaceful _____
15. glad, cheerful, content _____
16. smart, intelligent, brainy _____

HAIR-RAISING SYNONYMS

For each adjective on the left there is a compound synonym on the right. Pair them up correctly.

frightening, disturbing	**hair-raising**	big-headed
mean		cold-blooded
stubborn, obstinate		high-handed
excitable		open-minded
tolerant, even-tempered		muddle-headed
conceited, vain, boastful		tight-fisted
unemotional, unfeeling		**hair-raising**
cheerful, happy		narrow-minded
arrogant, presumptuous		highly-strung
wealthy, rich		easy-going
gentle, loving		well-balanced
considerate, receptive		absent-minded
unreasonable, bigoted		well-heeled
woolly, confused		pig-headed
insincere, hypocritical		slow-witted
stable, sensible		two-faced
stupid		light-hearted
forgetful, inattentive		kind-hearted

OF COMPOUNDS

Many compounds (fixed expressions made up of two words to express a new meaning) combine two nouns with the help of the preposition 'of', e.g. *rule of law, coat of arms, man of honour*. Pair up the elements in the grey box by combining them with 'of' and form compounds that complete the sentences below.

bird	end	point	stroke		art	life	mind	the town
code	guest	presence	talk	**of**	birth	**living**	prey	the world
cost	head	right	way		conduct	luck	state	view
date	name	state	work		honour	mind	the game	way

1. I'd like to move to London, but the _____**cost of living**_____ in big cities is just too high.

2. What a _____! I found that my new boss is an old school friend.

3. Before he recovered from his nervous breakdown, Ray was in a terrible _____.

4. The eagle is maybe the most majestic _____.

5. Most identity cards contain the person's _____.

6. Don't make such a fuss about this broken cup. It's not the _____, you know.

7. Whenever this film star is in London, she is the _____.

8. The 'Mona Lisa' is maybe the most well-known _____ on earth.

9. The Queen is the _____ of England, Scotland, Wales and Northern Ireland.

10. The _____ at this year's banquet will be the Minister of Education.

11. I had to stop my car, because the oncoming traffic had the _____.

12. The car came straight at Tom, but Sue had the _____ to drag him to safety.

13. Many people admire the American _____.

14. In a democracy everybody has a right to their own _____.

15. To make money is the _____ if you are in banking and investment.

16. Doctors must be guided by a strict _____ when treating patients.

Phrasal verbs (combinations of verb + adverb or preposition) have an idiomatic meaning all of their own, which cannot be guessed from their separate parts, e.g. *to look after = to care for*. *Look* is a verb which is used in many phrasal verbs. Write the definitions from the grey box next to the appropriate phrase. Then use the phrasal verbs with *look* to complete the sentences below. Don't forget to choose the correct tense forms.

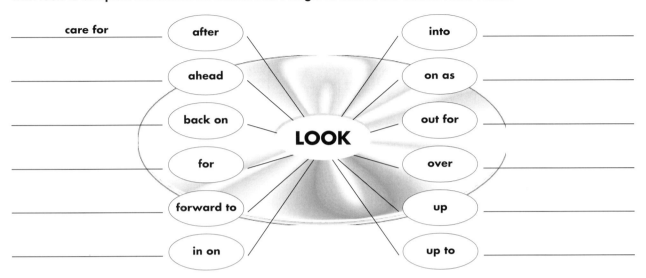

consider, think of as • examine quickly • examine in detail, investigate • expect in an optimistic mood
find out something (usually from a book, list, etc.) • pay attention to • remember • respect, admire • search
make plans for the future • **care for, be responsible for** • pay a visit (short and mostly unplanned)

1. The trouble with many young people is that they live for the moment and don't _____ .

2. _____ the new Spielberg film. It's really very good.

3. The committee is _____ the government's new tax proposals.

4. Where have you been? We've been _____ you all over the place.

5. We are all greatly _____ Peter's party on Saturday.

6. Our friends were passing through our town and decided to _____ us.

7. Our neighbours will be _____ our cat while we are on holiday.

8. I can never remember Tom's address. I always have to _____ it _____ .

9. My mother has many excellent qualities, she really is a person you can _____ .

10. We always _____ that stay with you with great pleasure.

11. We have always _____ Freya _____ a very special friend.

12. The professor merely had to _____ the essay to see that it was too short.

Why didn't you come and pick me up? Didn't you see the note I left you?

Homographs

Homographs are words which are written in the same way but have different meanings and sometimes also are pronounced differently. Complete the sentences with the homographs from the grey box.

| bar | bark | lead | live | match | **note** | party |
| race | rest | ring | row | spring | tank | tap |

The singer could not reach that high	**note**	at last night's concert.
Before going out Lisa wrote a		for her husband.
We drank from a little mountain		The water was delicious.
I think that of all the seasons it is		I like best.
I heard a soft		on the door and opened it.
The		in the kitchen is leaking.
I'll give you a		at the office as soon as I get back.
Mr Rockgiver bought a beautiful		for his wife.
This car has quite a large petrol		which holds 70 litres.
The use of the		in warfare dates back to World War I.
Have you got a		to light the candle?
Did you see that football		on TV last night?
A furious		started when Mr Smith came home.
They are building a		of new houses at the end of our road.
Don't mind Jim. His		is worse than his bite.
A tree's		is home to thousands of insects.
After a good		we continued with our work.
I will remember this holiday for the		of my life.
Tex went straight to the		and ordered a whisky.
Many children like a		of chocolate between meals.
The athlete won the		and received a medal.
Discrimination on the grounds of		is illegal.
I don't think any political		is able to solve today's problems.
Our neighbours had a noisy		last night.
Liverpool have just scored again and		by three goals to nil.
Cars with catalytic converters must use		-free petrol.
Gary Crooner always sings		on television.
It is my dream to		on an island in the South Sea one day.

Homophones
Put a Not in it!

A homophone (from Greek 'homo'=same and phoné=sound) is a word which sounds the same as another word, but has a different meaning. Homophones are often used in advertisements to create a humorous or memorable effect as in the anti-smoking advertisement above, which plays on the homophony of *'knot'* and *'not'*.

1. FIND THE TWO HOMOPHONES IN EACH LINE. USE A DICTIONARY TO CHECK WORDS YOU DON'T KNOW.

hair	here	hare	her		too	true	tow	toe
no	know	knew	now		sale	sole	sail	salt
moat	mate	meet	meat		raise	rose	rows	rouse
slow	sleigh	slay	sly		threw	throw	through	trough
moon	moan	mown	mean		same	some	sum	seem
mile	male	mail	mole		soul	sale	sold	sole
loan	line	lane	lone		brake	broke	break	brace
ride	rate	rite	right		wade	weight	weighed	wide

2. FILL IN THE BLANKS IN EACH SENTENCE WITH HOMOPHONE PAIRS FROM THE GREY BOX.

ate	blew	son	eight	for	rode	two	here	too
hear	road	four	sea	right	see	blue	sun	write

1. I would _____ her a letter, but I haven't got the _____ address.

2. As we came towards the coast we could _____ the _____ .

3. Looking _____ the right way, the _____ riders _____ down the _____ .

4. I was so hungry that I _____ _____ pieces of pizza.

5. Thank you, one whiskey is enough, _____ would be _____ much.

6. My _____ always goes to Spain because he loves the _____ .

7. The wind _____ away the clouds and we had a clear _____ sky.

8. If you come over _____ you can _____ the waterfall.

25

'For better for worse, for richer for poorer, in sickness and in health'

FOR *B*ETTER FOR WORSE

*A*n antonym is a word which means the opposite, or nearly the opposite, of another word. 'Rich and poor', and 'Sickness and health' are antonyms, but so are 'husband and wife', 'bride and bridegroom'. Two of the words in each line are antonyms. Circle them and explain in what way they are opposites.

(soft)	slow	(hard)	nice
medium	strong	weak	tired
shy	quiet	poor	bold
short	tall	great	huge
narrow	wide	long	high
crispy	hot	soggy	clean
bitter	sweet	crunchy	tough
quiet	dark	pretty	noisy
small	common	rare	afraid
first	second	middle	last

remember	criticise	praise	invite
steal	read	borrow	lend
arrive	stay	leave	begin
conclude	win	play	lose
remember	forget	think	understand
beg	ask	respond	reject
admire	show	see	detest
do	stay	build	destroy
start	move	improve	finish
keep	sell	buy	give

Choose from the antonym-pairs above and write ten sentences; you must use <u>both</u> words in each sentence.

_____

_____

_____

_____

_____

_____

_____

DOUBLE ANTONYMS

As some words can have more than one meaning (or different shades of meaning) they also have more than one antonym, the opposite of *SOFT music*, for example, is *LOUD music*, but the opposite of a *SOFT surface* is a *HARD surface*. For each of the adjectives in fat print below there are two opposites in the grey box. Find them and write them next to the given nouns. Be clear about their precise meaning, however, as each antonym can only be combined with one of the given nouns.

artificial	bad	bright	correct	easy	evil	famous	fat
feeble	Happy	**hard**	interesting	large	light	**loud**	Merry
notorious	sharp	soft	synthetic	tall	thick	true	weak

soft
_____**loud**_____ music
_____**hard**_____ surface

dark
_____ hair
_____ stars

good
_____ spirit
_____ example

natural
_____ light
_____ fibres

sad
_____ Christmas!
_____ Birthday!

dull
_____ knife
_____ story

unknown
_____ film star
_____ criminal

strong
_____ coffee
_____ mind

small
_____ tree
_____ country

false
_____ friend
_____ address

thin
_____ coat
_____ cheque

hard
_____ task
_____ wood

MAKING HEADLINES

*E*nglish newspaper headlines, particularly those of the popular papers, have developed a style and vocabulary of their own. To attract the reader's attention they use short rather than long words (for example wed, bid and plea instead of marry, attempt and request), abbreviations (£4m instead of four million pounds) and clippings (lab for laboratory, doc for doctor, etc.).

Pair up the headlines below with the texts on the opposite page.

1. Row over UFO riddle
2. MPs BACK DRIVE TO AXE DRUG LAWS
3. Boss quits, weds PA
4. TOP DOC IN BOOZE OP CLASH
5. PEACE TALKS HIT BY BOMB BLAST
6. KEY PROBE LINKS KIDS' TELLY HABITS TO SCHOOL AGGRO
7. Hol mum in cab shock
8. PM VOWS TO FIGHT JOB CUTS
9. £ BOOSTS HOPES FOR JOBLESS
10. Queen wows O.A.P.s

Headline: 7
The 35-year-old mother of three had come back from a holiday and was horrified when the taxi driver asked her for £ 50 for . . .

Headline:
People in the pretty village of Saxby in East Anglia have come into conflict over the mystery of some strange 'landing marks' in a nearby cornfield, which some villagers claim have been caused by Unidentified Flying Objects from outer space . . .

Headline:
A group of senior Members of Parliament yesterday announced their support for the campaign to remove the legal penalties for the possession of small amounts of cannabis.

Headline:
. . . The expectations for a fall in the number of unemployed people is based on the strong performance of the pound . . .

Headline:
The Prime Minister promised a new plan that will make it harder for firms to reduce staff. In a . . .

Headline:
. . . walkabout. The monarch filled old age pensioners with delight when she came over and started to talk to them . . .

Headline:
. . . the discussions on a lasting agreement between the two warring factions suffered a severe setback after an explosion near the hotel ripped open . . .

Headline:
. . . dispute over a group of leading doctors' suggestion to ban people who drink a lot of alcohol from live-saving liver transplant operations is growing . . .

Headline:
. . . This is the most comprehensive and important investigation ever, and it shows that there is a clear connection between what children and adolescents watch on television and aggressive behaviour in the classroom . . .

Headline:
Andrew Marshal, 54, chairman of Byte Electronics, said that it was time to leave and announced that he was going to marry his Personal Assistant, Mrs Sarah Mayle. The happy couple . . .

NOW PAIR UP THE HEADLINE WORDS WITH THE EQUIVALENT WORDS OR PHRASES FROM THE TEXTS

row _____

UFO _____

riddle _____

MPs _____

back _____

drive _____

axe _____

boss _____

quit _____

wed _____

PA _____

top _____

doc _____

booze _____

op _____

clash _____

talks _____

hit _____

blast _____

key _____

probe _____

link _____

kids _____

telly _____

aggro _____

hol _____

mum _____

cab _____

PM _____

vow _____

cut _____

£ _____

hopes _____

jobless _____

wow _____

OAPs _____

CONFUSABLE ADJECTIVES

In the first column are some adjectives which often are confused because they have similar but not identical meanings. Choose the correct words to go with the sentences in the second column. Use your dictionary to find out about the differences in meaning.

LAST / LATEST

Elizabeth Buchan's _____ book is called 'Perfect Love'.

Melissa is crazy about the _____ fashion.

During the _____ five years, I have only been to Paris once.

BIG / LARGE / GREAT

Napoleon was not a tall man, but he was a _____ man.

Mr Bryson was holding a _____ black umbrella in his hand.

Behind the house there is a _____ garden.

ILL / SICK

My mother has been seriously _____ for weeks now.

The other day someone was _____ on the bus. What a smell!

LUCKY / HAPPY

I was _____ to hear that you arrived safely.

He was very _____ . The job might have gone to somebody else.

FOREIGN / STRANGE

Did you hear that _____ noise in the living-room?

About five million _____ visitors come to England every year.

HIGH / TALL

Mrs Simmons wears high heels to make herself look _____ .

Herr Huber lives in the _____ mountains of southern Germany.

From the road we could see the _____ walls of the famous prison.

ALIVE / LIVING / LIVELY

I know his father is still _____ and living somewhere in Scotland.

We had a very _____ conversation about animal rights last night.

I have no _____ relatives left now.

SYMPATHETIC / FRIENDLY

During my recent illness, Joan was very _____ and understanding.

The people in Britain are so _____ towards foreigners!

QUIET / QUITE

This is _____ a large house. Isn't it too _____ here?

LITTLE / SHORT / SMALL

Mr Pintsize is a _____ man. He barely comes up to my shoulders.

What a pity that this nice _____ house is too _____ for us.

BRIEFLY / SHORTLY

My mother and Mrs Taylor had met _____ once before.

_____ after the meal I was taken ill and driven to the hospital.

When my aunt returned, I told her _____ what had happened.

HUMAN / HUMANE

As the _____ body grows, it develops many skills.

All people in the world belong to the _____ race.

The mental asylum treated their patients in a very _____ way.

SENSIBLE / SENSITIVE

Why don't you make a _____ decision for once, you fool!

Please be careful what you say, he's so _____ about his nose.

She told him to act like a brave and _____ man.

It's not a good idea to read ghost stories to _____ children at night.

ACTUAL / PRESENT / TOPICAL

I'm not exaggerating, those were his _____ words!

Something that is _____ concerns events that are happening at the _____ time.

EVENTUALLY / POSSIBLY

After a long discussion we _____ came to a decision.

I'm going to London tomorrow and may _____ meet him then.

COMIC / COMICAL

All clowns like wearing _____ hats.

Don't you think there's something slightly _____ about him?

ECONOMIC / ECONOMICAL

It's not easy to find a job in the present _____ climate.

In times of crises people have to be as _____ as possible.

ELECTRIC / ELECTRICAL

Switch on the _____ fire in the study, please!

My father is an _____ engineer.

An _____ plug is designed to carry electricity.

Do you have any _____ appliances in your kitchen?

AMERICAN ENGLISH

It has been said that America and Great Britain are two great countries divided by a common language. In 1939 the author of an American-English Dictionary wrote that 'an American, if suddenly ill on a visit to London, might die in the street because nobody would know what he meant when he asked for the nearest drugstore.' Well, all Americans can feel quite safe now. The constant interchange through the mass media, business, science, technology and travel has brought the two forms of English together again. As a matter of fact, it is getting more and more difficult to make a clear distinction between them.

There are, however, hundreds of words that are used differently on the two sides of the Atlantic, e.g. the different parts of a car.

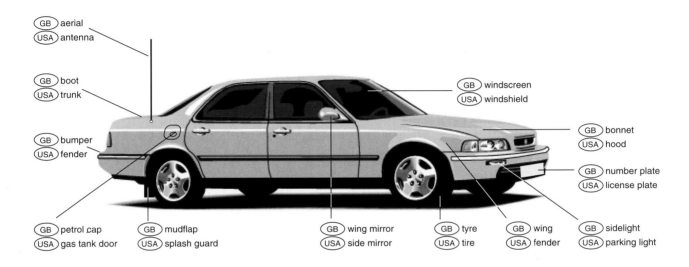

PAIR THEM UP!

The words on the left are American English, the words on the right British English. Pair them up correctly.

apartment	motorway	can (for food)	post code
baggage	pavement	French fries	holiday
candy	underground	line	railway
cookie	luggage	pants	lorry
elevator	front garden	railroad	queue
fall	flat	station wagon	tin
freeway	sweets	trash	chips
sidewalk	biscuit	truck	trousers
subway	lift	vacation	rubbish
yard	autumn	zip code	estate car

WHAT'S COOKING?

American English has also greatly enriched the language with many colourful and memorable idiomatic expressions. Use the following to complete the sentences below.

> to bark up the wrong tree • to get even (with someone)
>
> to face the music • to fill the bill • to make a bee-line (for)
>
> to get away with (something) • to get hot under the collar
>
> to hit the road • to knock the socks off (someone/something)
>
> to jump on the bandwagon • to make one's mind up
>
> to take it easy • to play hardball • to sit on the fence

1. It's getting late, I suppose it's time for me to _____ .

2. I was so hungry that I _____ for the fridge as soon as I got home.

3. No, I told you I didn't do it, you are _____ .

4. Al had an accident in his father's car and has just gone home to _____ .

5. You can't just _____ . Someday you'll have to make a decision.

6. Don't _____ . Calm down!

7. If we want to succeed we must stop fooling around and start to _____ .

8. Don't just sit here and be angry. Fight back. You know what they say, 'Don't get mad, _____ .'

9. Michael Jackson still _____ all those other singers.

10. Well, do you want to marry Janet or Joanne? You must _____ someday.

11. When they saw that cutting taxes was popular, all the other parties _____ .

12. What made you think you could _____ such a stupid lie?

13. On a hot day like this a nice cool beer exactly _____ .

14. Don't worry, everything will be fine, you'll see. Just _____ .

NOW YOU'RE TALKING!

Choose the correct questions or replies from the grey box and insert them where appropriate.

> I'll pick you up about 7.30.
> Are you sure it's not too much trouble?
> Yes, I think I'll have a piece of cheese cake.
> Hello. This is Sue. May I speak to Jim, please?
> Very little milk without sugar, please.
> I'm afraid I've broken one of your mugs.
> No, thank you. I'll ring back later.
> I'm ever so sorry. Won't you let me replace it?
> I'm afraid I didn't quite hear what you said.
> Do you feel like going to the cinema this evening?
> A cup of tea for me, please.
> Yes, much better than yesterday, isn't it?

ON THE TELEPHONE

a. Folkestone 54854

b. _____

a. He's out, I'm afraid. Can I take a message?

b. _____

a. All right. Bye.
b. Bye.

ASKING PEOPLE OUT

a. _____

b. I'd like that very much. Thank you.

a. _____

b. Fine. See you then.

ASKING PEOPLE TO REPEAT THINGS

a. _____

b. I said 'Can I give you a lift home?'

a. _____

b. No, it's on my way home. Come on, jump in!

WITH A FRIEND IN A CAFE

a. What can I get you to drink?

b. _____

a. How do you like it?

b. _____

a. Do you fancy something to eat?

b. _____

a. Right, I'll bring it over to our table.

APOLOGISING

a. _____

b. Oh, don't worry about that.

a. _____

b. Certainly not. I wouldn't dream of letting you do that.

TALKING ABOUT THE WEATHER

a. It seems to be clearing up.

b. _____

a. Apparently it's going to turn warmer.

b. Oh. That would make a change, wouldn't it?

Is it too far to walk?
Just black coffee, please.
Excuse me, please, but I'm trying to find the Tower.
That's quite all right.
Yes, I'll have soup of the day to start with.
I really must be going now.
I think I'll try the vegetable curry, please.

That's very kind of you, but I mustn't be too late.
Thank you very much for a lovely evening.
Can I help you?
How much is it, please?
Anything else?
When are you leaving?
Have a safe journey. Don't forget to write to us.

IN A RESTAURANT

a. May I take your order, Sir?

b. _____

a. And to follow?

b. _____

a. Any dessert?

b. _____

ASKING THE WAY

a. _____

b. Turn right, across the bridge. You can't miss it.

a. _____

b. No, it's only about five minutes' walk.

a. Thank you very much.

b. _____

SAYING GOODBYE

a. I've just called in to say goodbye.

b. _____

a. I'm flying home tomorrow morning.

b. _____

a. Thanks, come and see me if ever you're in Berlin.

THANKING FOR HOSPITALITY

a. _____

b. So soon? Won't you have another drink?

a. _____

b. What a shame!

a. _____

b. I'm glad you enjoyed it. Hope you can come again.

SHOPPING

a. _____

b. I'd like a large tin of cat food, please.

a. I'm afraid we've only got the small size left.

b. _____

a. Seventy pence.

b. All right. I'll have two, please.

a. _____

b. No, thank you. That's all.

MIXED BAG QUIZ

Tick the boxes with the corrrect answers.

This man is . . . a photograph.
- making
- picturing
- taking
- drawing

Which person is present at a tennis match?
- a judge
- a referee
- an examiner
- an umpire

Three babies born at the same time are
- triplets
- triangles
- tripods
- triceps

An American calls it an elevator; in Britain it is
- a lift
- an escalator
- a staircase
- a radiator

What are lines on the face called?
- creases
- folds
- pleats
- wrinkles

This girl has a ... headache.
- dividing
- screeching
- cutting
- splitting

If you turn your back on people, you
- ignore them
- back them
- support them
- want to go home

The most exciting part of a story is its
- summit
- peak
- top
- climax

If you want to make your house bigger, you...it
- inflate
- grow
- extend
- increase

Where would you find a congregation, an aisle and an altar?
- in a hospital
- in a garage
- in a church
- in an office

Which person pays rent?
- a landlord
- a tenant
- a proprietor
- an owner

A fisherman uses ....
- equipment
- apparatus
- appliances
- tackle

and a surgeon uses surgical ....
- instruments
- tools
- implements
- utensils

What sort of person would you call a shark?
- a good swimmer
- a murderer
- a crook
- a whale lover

When a train does not arrive in time, it's
- postponed
- belated
- delayed
- retarded

What is the time between day and night called?
- dusk
- obscurity
- gloom
- dark

Which one of these would you use to move leaves?
- a scoop
- a rake
- a fork
- a shovel

Which professional group do you associate with the words extraction, drilling and filling?
- dentists
- doctors
- scientists
- opticians

Which of these words is least strong?
- to loathe
- to dislike
- to hate
- to detest

The words hammer, screwdriver and electric drill all have something to do with
- shapes
- health care
- tools
- clothes

36

Look for Links

| Day is to sun as night is to | ○ dawn | ✖ moon | ○ sleep | ○ dusk |

Choose the correct word to complete the sentences as in the example above.

1. Bear is to animal as bush is to — ○ plant ○ tree ○ vegetable ○ insect
2. Eye is to see as nose is to — ○ notice ○ smell ○ hear ○ hand
3. Author is to book as painter is to — ○ museum ○ sculpture ○ music ○ picture
4. Loud is to shout as quiet is to — ○ silent ○ whisper ○ talk ○ scream
5. Man is to talk as horse is to — ○ bray ○ sing ○ neigh ○ shout
6. Bee is to honey as cow is to — ○ milk ○ bull ○ grass ○ cream
7. Sheep is to lamb as dog is to — ○ puppy ○ foal ○ kid ○ calf
8. Summer is to winter as hot is to — ○ spring ○ autumn ○ warm ○ cold
9. Thought is to think as caught is to — ○ game ○ rope ○ play ○ catch
10. Mouse is to mice as child is to — ○ cat ○ rat ○ children ○ boy
11. Often is to always as seldom is to — ○ sometimes ○ never ○ ever ○ frequently
12. Gloves are to hands as socks are to — ○ shoes ○ knees ○ feet ○ legs
13. Two is to hands as ten is to — ○ toes ○ hands ○ thumbs ○ feet
14. Swim is to water as fly is to — ○ bathe ○ land ○ plane ○ air
15. Up is to down as top is to — ○ centre ○ side ○ bottom ○ left
16. Ear is to hearing as mouth is to — ○ face ○ teeth ○ taste ○ lips

Look in the Right Place

You'll find a doctor in a hospital, and a teacher in a . . .

Pair up the words that belong together in each column.

1	astronomer	**observatory**	T.V. studio
2	bell		embassy
3	cashier		university
4	check-out		gymnasium
5	dentist		fairground
6	diplomat		prison
7	fruit tree		hotel
8	grave		bank
9	mechanic		**observatory**
10	newsreader		surgery
11	painting		clock tower
12	professor		orchard
13	reception		supermarket
14	roller coaster		gallery
15	sports teacher		cemetery
16	warden		garage

LANDMARKS

Reunite the famous international landmarks, countries and geographical features below by pairing up the missing words in the grey box with their first parts.

Arabia	Constance	Islands	Sea
Bridge	Desert	Lakes	States
Canyon	Forest	Mexico	Tower
Channel	House	Ocean	Tunnel
China	Ireland	Palace	Zealand

The Great Wall of _____

The Baltic _____

Lake _____

Golden Gate _____

The English _____

The United _____

The Sahara _____

The Black _____

The Grand _____

The Pacific _____

The Eiffel _____

Buckingham _____

Saudi _____

Galapagos _____

The White _____

The Republic of _____

New _____

The Channel _____

The Great _____

The Gulf of _____

Now write one (or more) sentence(s) about each of the landmarks you have found.

39

KNOW THE INs AND OUTs

Someone who *knows the ins and outs* of something knows it very well.

Phrasal verbs are combinations of verb + adverb or verb + preposition; they have an idiomatic meaning all of their own, which cannot be guessed from their separate parts. IN and OUT are two particles which appear in many phrasal verbs.

Use the verbs in the grey box to complete the sentences with the correct phrasals. Watch the tenses.

back	call	count	fall	settle	step
bring	**check**	cut	fill	sell	turn
break	clear	drop	set	sort	watch

1. The guests __**checked**__ in at the hotel reception.
2. You promised to help us. You can't _____ out now.
3. Okay, I'll join your team; you can _____ me in.
4. The prisoners who _____ out of jail yesterday have all been caught.
5. Why does John always have to _____ in when other people are talking?
6. Dad promised me ten pounds if I _____ out the garden shed for him.
7. I don't normally work here; I'm just _____ in for a colleague on holiday.
8. Dave and Fay have _____ out with each other and haven't been talking for a week.
9. Why don't you _____ in when you're in the area?
10. I'm on a diet, so I have to _____ out for those hidden fats in my food.
11. It was such a lovely morning, but in the afternoon the rain _____ in.
12. Mr Troubleshooter will soon have _____ out all those problems in our firm.
13. The football hooligans started brawling, but the police immediately _____ in.
14. The man at the door _____ out to be a police detective.
15. How is Peter _____ in at his new school?
16. I am sorry, but we are _____ out, we haven't got a single loaf of bread left.
17. Our washing machine didn't work and we had to _____ in a service man.
18. Working on a difficult task often _____ out the best in people.

GET YOUR TEETH INTO COLLOQUIAL ENGLISH

In everyday English people often use informal expressions, which exist 'below' the accepted formal standard – you would not use them in a serious piece of writing or in a formal speech; at the same time they are by no means part of slang, i.e. they are quite acceptable expressions. English is full of such colourful and lively expressions. Complete the sentences with the colloquial expressions from the grey box; make changes where necessary.

call it a day	have a go at something	promise the earth
draw a blank	laugh your head off	pull out all the stops
get the hang of something	live it up	**pull somebody's leg**
give somebody the once-over	pass the buck	stick around
turn a blind eye	perk up	take it easy

1. Have you really won in the lottery or are you just **pulling my leg** ?
2. Okay, let's _____ . We can finish tomorrow.
3. I saw my friend make a mistake but I _____ .
4. It's always the same when something goes wrong. Everybody just tries to _____ .
5. We've really _____ this Christmas. We've decorated the whole house.
6. The star's bodyguard _____ the journalist _____ and let him in.
7. We saw an incredibly funny film yesterday evening. We were all _____ .
8. I thought I might find Emma at home, but I _____ .
9. I was tired all morning, but after lunch I suddenly _____ .
10. I quite like my new job, but it took some time to _____ .
11. Could you _____ till Susan comes back? I'm sure she'd love to see you.
12. We went to a different party every night, we were really _____ .
13. Politicians usually _____ before an election.
14. Let Pete _____ at mending the radio, I'm sure he can do it.
15. After an operation like this you should _____ for a while.

41

Just like a bull in a china shop...

'**To be like a bull in a china shop**' is an **idiom of comparison**. English is rich in short comparisons which make the language and conversation more interesting and vivid. The expressions below are used in informal everyday English. Try to make out the correct definitions and then go on to the next page to learn some more.

Sue and Sean get on like a house on fire

- ○ They like each other and get on extremely well
- ○ They both have a fiery temperament but love each other
- ○ They both work for the fire brigade
- ○ They live in the same house

Jenny has taken to her new computer like a duck to water

- ○ She finds typing on the computer very difficult
- ○ She is naturally good at working with the computer and likes it very much
- ○ She doesn't like the ducks showing on the screen
- ○ She always liked computers

He felt like a fish out of water at that trendy party last night

- ○ It had been raining and he arrived all soaked and cold
- ○ He felt uncomfortable and out of place. The surroundings were so unfamiliar to him
- ○ He felt thirsty and nobody offered him a drink
- ○ He didn't know anyone

Dave slept like a log last night!

- ○ He had to sleep in a wooden bed last night
- ○ He slept very uncomfortably last night
- ○ He slept very deeply and continuously last night

The girls treated Fay like dirt

- ○ The girls treated Fay unfairly and with no respect
- ○ The girls talked behind Fay's back all the time
- ○ The other girls did not want to make friends with Fay

Carol went out like a light

- ○ She was so tired that she fell asleep immediately
- ○ Before going to bed she switched all the lights off
- ○ She went out in a very light dress because it was so warm

John's wife keeps telling him to redecorate the children's bedroom, but her suggestions are like water off a duck's back

- ○ Her suggestions have no effect at all. John doesn't take any notice
- ○ She has chosen wallpaper with a duck pattern and John doesn't want to put it up
- ○ John doesn't know how to decorate a room
- ○ John says that they can't afford to redecorate the room

IDIOMS OF COMPARISON

*P*air up the idioms in the grey box with the definitions; then use them to complete the sentences below.

like a bolt from the blue	like a bull in a china shop	like cat and dog
like a bear with a sore head	like a sore thumb	like hot cakes
like a sieve	like the back of your hand	like a red rag to a bull
like a ton of bricks	like wildfire	like a glove

A. If something spreads very quickly, it spreads _____

B. If something is certain to make someone very angry, it's _____

C. If someone is extremely clumsy, he or she is _____

D. If a piece of news comes unexpectedly, it comes _____

E. If something fits exactly, it fits _____

F. Someone who forgets things easily has a memory _____

G. If you know something extremely well, you know it _____

H. If people are fighting or disagreeing violently, they fight _____

I. If things are selling very well and quickly, they sell _____

J. Something that's very conspicuous, and usually inappropriate, sticks out _____

K. If someone is very bad-tempered and irritable, he or she is _____

L. If you reprimand or criticise someone sharply or severely, you come down on them _____

1. It's a pity this sweatshirt is the wrong colour because it fits _____ .

2. My Dad never remembers my Mum's birthday. He's got a memory _____ .

3. If my mother ever finds out that I lied, she will come down on me _____ .

4. Please don't wear that hat to the party. You'll stick out _____ !

5. I was too late to do anything about it. The rumour spread _____ .

6. Why don't you cheer up? You've been _____ for the past two days!

7. This is the best invention since sliced bread! The games are selling _____ !

8. Mentioning animal rights to my uncle is _____ . He's a butcher.

9. My younger sisters don't get on at all. They are always fighting _____ .

10. Jack has been a London cabbie for years. He knows the city _____ .

11. Stop being so uncoordinated and careless! You're just _____ .

12. The news of his mother's sudden illness came _____ .

43

FIXED PHRASES

A fixed phrase is a combination of an adjective and a noun, which functions as a single word referring to a single particular person, object or idea; you can therefore find these combinations in a dictionary. Pair up the nouns and adjectives correctly, then use the fixed phrases to complete the sentences below.

alarm • breakdown • business • cow • delivery • **drink** • heating
home • motion • order • pages • play • property • transport • twins

alcoholic **drink**	identical _____	sacred _____
big _____	mobile _____	slow _____
central _____	nervous _____	special _____
false _____	private _____	standing _____
foul _____	public _____	yellow _____

1. Important documents should always be sent by _____.
2. A _____ at your bank is the best way to pay your rent each month.
3. Please keep out. This garden is _____.
4. They are _____ and sometimes you really can't tell them apart.
5. When the police found the body, they immediately suspected _____.
6. It is fascinating to watch the movements of a tennis player in _____ on TV.
7. In parts of America you cannot buy an _____ if you are under 21.
8. The fire-brigade arrived very quickly, but it had only been a _____.
9. Trains and buses are the most widespread means of _____.
10. A _____ is a large movable caravan which people live in.
11. Everybody talks about wage restraint, but directors' salaries seem to be a _____.
12. In some countries illegal drugs have become _____.
13. Where can I get this picture framed? – Why don't you look in the _____?
14. _____ is a good thing, but the air often gets very dry in the rooms.
15. We've had so much work at the office lately that the boss had a _____.

44

UP OR DOWN?

Write the explanations in the grey box next to the appropriate phrasal verbs. Then use the phrasal verbs to complete the sentences below. Take care to choose the correct tense forms.

Explanation	Phrasal verb	Phrasal verb	Explanation
educate a child	bring up	close down	
	look up to	settle down	
	make up	bring down	
	mix up	pull down	
	put up	let down	
	put up with	pour down	
	shut up	turn down	

admire, respect • be quiet, stop talking • build, erect • confuse • disappoint
demolish • invent, create • live a regular, quiet life • **raise, educate children**
rain very hard • reduce • refuse • shut, cease to operate • tolerate, accept

1. Mr May has just _____ his garage, he is going to _____ a greenhouse instead.
2. Pam still _____ her brother, although he has _____ her _____ so many times.
3. It was _____ all day, so we stayed at home.
4. The introduction of the seat belt has _____ the number of road deaths.
5. During the recession a lot of shops had to _____ .
6. Jack asked Jill to marry him, but she _____ him _____ .
7. I wish Tim would _____ ; he's talking such nonsense.
8. Mandy travelled all over the world, but now she has _____ in a quiet Devon village.
9. I'm not prepared to _____ Ray's stupid behaviour any more.
10. Carla _____ her children to recognise right from wrong.
11. This writer _____ very good stories for children.
12. My sister and I look very much alike and people often _____ us _____ .

All's WELL THAT ENDS WELL

Choose from the words in the grey box to complete the words in each group.

bed • **board** • boat • book • house • light • line • paper
pot • room • ship • side • way • word • work

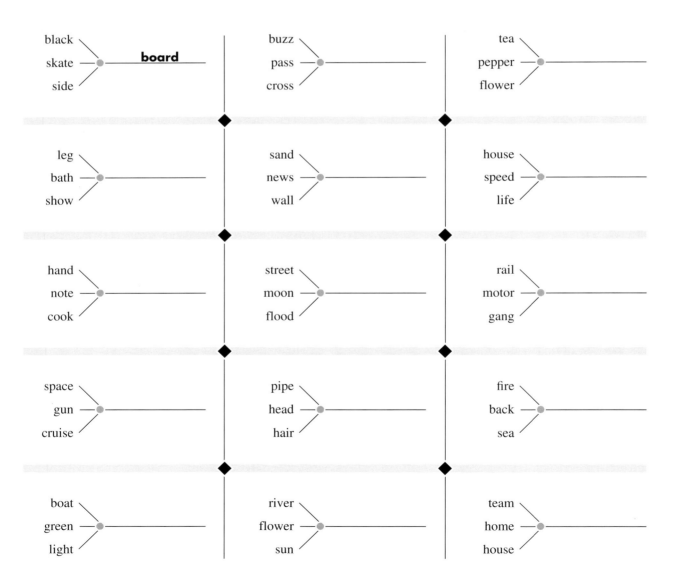

LADIES AND GENTLEMEN!

Like 'Ladies and Gentlemen' there are many fixed phrases linked by 'and' and always used in a certain fixed order, e.g. 'Ladies and Gentlemen', never 'Gentlemen and Ladies'. Pair up the elements in the grey box by combining them with 'and', forming expressions that complete the sentences below.

bed	drinking	law	rock	*a*	blood	easy	**low**	quiet
bits	facts	life	rules	*n*	breakfast	figures	night	regulations
day	flesh	nice	sick		death	fun	order	roll
dead	**high**	peace	sun	*d*	driving	gone	pieces	tired

1. Wherever have you been? I've been searching for you _____**high and low**_____.

2. Dad built this shelf from _____ he found in the garden shed.

3. I had worried a lot about my exams, but it all went _____.

4. I'm _____ of all this horrible rap music on the radio.

5. _____ is one of the major causes of traffic accidents.

6. Before we make a decision we must get in the latest _____.

7. Some people say tough _____ politics are the only way to fight crime.

8. Gary Puller had a smashing time on one of those _____ holidays.

9. My firm have very strict _____ with regard to safety.

10. I wonder what the world will look like in a hundred year's time when I'm _____.

11. My brother called me a liar. I didn't expect this from my own _____.

12. This weekend, I will just sit in the garden and enjoy the _____.

13. Elvis Presley is often called the king of _____.

14. You must report this incident to the police. It may be a _____ situation.

15. I'm so exhausted. I've been working on that project _____.

16. Many tourists in England prefer _____ accommodation to a hotel.

Shark Reef

Visit a unique coral reef teeming with man-eating sharks. Observe and photograph these amazing creatures at close range while our divemasters feed them. You won't believe your eyes as the man-eating monsters of the deep sink their razor-sharp teeth into pieces of fish just inches away from our divers' bodies.

Your friends won't believe you when you show them your photos, so we'll give you a certificate as proof that you've got what it takes to come face to face with one of the most ferocious creatures on this planet.

Every dive is an action-packed adventure and unforgettable experience. Divers come from all over the world to witness this strange undersea phenomenon and feel the thrill and the shudder of the most extraordinary dive of the century.

▶ We now interrupt this book for a short commercial break!

BAVARIA!

Come to the country where views and values have changed little with the passage of time. Relax and breathe freely in the peace of our glorious landscape – gentle meadows dotted with cows peacefully grazing against the snow-capped backdrop of the majestic Alps. Let the romance of King Ludwig's fairy-tale castles and the baroque splendour of our monasteries and churches weave their magic on you and transport you to the timeless quality of peaceful country living.

Friendly people offer you a warm welcome. Join the locals when they yodel and play their merry oompah music in the market-place.

Taste the traditional local specialities in our many restaurants and gemütlich beer-gardens. There is something for every taste and every pocket and children are welcome everywhere.

THE BEST TOMATO EVER!

This new Tomato that will revolutionize home gardening – a breakthrough that someday will be in everyone's garden. But if you act quickly, you can be one of the **FIRST** gardeners to grow it now! Let others follow where you lead!

INCREDIBLY DELICIOUS TASTE! – This fabulous Tomato is the all-time champ. Its ruby-red flesh bursts forth with juicy goodness, mouthwatering flavour and an intense delicious taste. Each super-juicy fruit is a whopping 12 inches . . . 13 inches . . . 14 inches or more around.

Until you've enjoyed it for yourself, you simply cannot possibly imagine how absolutely delicious a Tomato can be! Just imagine the taste-thrills as you sink your teeth into these amazingly delicious mega-Tomatoes right off the bush!

HERO OF YOUR FAMILY! – You'll be the hero of your family, and the hit of your neighbourhood with these spectacular beauties! And you'll have more than enough to share with the neighbours . . . because I'm not talking skimpy. I'm talking Tomatoes . . . scores of Tomatoes! Not those teensy-weensy tiny Tomatoes other bushes produce, but big blockbuster superstar beauties.

BY APPOINTMENT
TO HER MAJESTY QUEEN ELIZABETH II

The best of Everything at Fortnum & Mason

It is more than 200 years since William Fortnum & Hugh Mason began trading in 1707, when 'High Quality' and 'The Best of Everything' became the watchwords of a success which continues to this present time.

Today, within this world-famous house the best of everything includes the finest foods and wine, exclusive fashions and perfumes, gifts in leather, antiques, china and glass and luxurious gifts of quality.

May it be that a long time from now we shall still be enjoying the same ideals.

Pride in Service since 1707

**Fortnum & Mason Ltd
Piccadilly, London**

1. What idea, message and image does each advertisement want to convey, whom are they addressed to and what responses do they want to evoke in the reader or listener?
2. Make lists of the words and expressions which are used to achieve these effects.

3. Read the texts aloud to give them their full flavour.

CREATIVE WRITING

1. You are the Creative Director of the agency which created the ads. Choose one of them as an example and explain to your clients the agency's choice of language and how you think it is going to be effective.
2. ADD YOUR AD! Write an advertisement for
   - your home town
   - your favourite kind of holiday
   - your favourite meal
   - yourself
   - an ideal place where you might want to live.
   - a real or imaginary product of your choice – a car, computer, holiday destination, fashion item, etc.

Who is Who?

English is very rich in colourful expressions describing character or the behaviour of someone in a certain situation. Choose from the following expressions to complete the characterisations below.

bully	couch potato	daredevil	fusspot	gatecrasher
heart-throb	night owl	nosey-parker	snob	spendthrift
stick-in-the-mud	rough diamond	stuffed shirt	wannabe	whizz-kid

1. A _____ is someone who spends most of his time at home watching TV.

2. A _____ has outwardly unpolished behaviour, but is at heart a good person.

3. A _____ doesn't want to try anything new, but always keeps to old routines.

4. A _____ is a man (often a film or pop star) who is very attractive.

5. A _____ sticks to the rules in a formal, self-important and inflexible way.

6. A _____ thinks that his tastes and manners are better than those of others.

7. A _____ uses his strength or power to frighten or hurt others.

8. A _____ is a person who spends money in a wasteful and stupid way.

9. A _____ is always complaining and very difficult to please.

10. A _____ tries to be like a film or rock star by imitating them.

11. A _____ wants to know things which are none of his business.

12. A _____ enjoys doing dangerous things.

13. A _____ comes to a party without having been invited.

14. A _____ habitually stays up late or likes to work at night.

15. A _____ is highly successful very quickly because of his / her clever ideas.

Think of people – real or imaginary – who fit these descriptions, describe their behaviour in typical situations.

GERUND COMPOUNDS

A sleeping tablet is not a tablet that has fallen asleep but a tablet that helps people go to sleep. In compounds like these the -ing-form is not an adjective but a gerund, which acts like a noun.
Make compounds by pairing up the elements in the grey box, then use them to complete the sentences.

boarding	eating	opening	sleeping		aid	**code**	ground	pass
breeding	hearing	playing	stumbling	+	bag	costs	gum	place
chewing	living	running	swimming		block	costume	habits	point
dialling	meeting	sailing	turning		boat	fields	night	room

1. I want to make a call to New York. Can you tell me the _____**dialling code**_____ for the US?

2. The family are all sitting in the _____ .

3. Tomorrow is the _____ for this year's summer concerts.

4. English public schools offer many sports and have excellent _____ .

5. The slums of Los Angeles are often seen as a _____ for crime.

6. My uncle is taking part in the regatta in his new _____ .

7. Some dentists say that _____ is good for your teeth.

8. Get your _____ ! We're going down to the beach.

9. If you go camping, you need a nice, warm _____ .

10. You'll need a _____ , if you want to get on this flight.

11. The biggest _____ for John's promotion is his lack of patience.

12. A Rolls Royce is a great car, but the _____ are just too high.

13. His marriage to Sue was the great _____ in Jim's life.

14. Look at Sloppy wolfing down a hamburger. His _____ are disgusting!

15. The French Riviera is the traditional _____ of the European jet set.

16. Since my uncle got his _____ , he can take part in every conversation.

51

Have a nice day!

Thank you, but I have other plans.

More American & British English

American English (AmE) and British English (BrE) sometimes have two different words for the same thing. Compile your own dictionary by choosing from the words below and writing them underneath the objects shown.

AMERICAN ENGLISH

adhesive tape • baby carriage • bill • billfold
buffet • cookies • faucet • French fries
pacifier • German shepherd • shades
truck • station wagon • street car • trailer
street musician • tic-tac-toe • trash can

BRITISH ENGLISH

Alsatian • bank note • biscuits • busker
caravan • chips • dummy • sideboard
dustbin • estate car • noughts and crosses
pram (perambulator) • sunglasses • tap
lorry • sticking plaster • tram • wallet

AmE _____

BrE _____

AmE _____

BrE _____

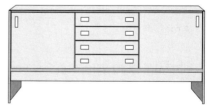

AmE _____

BrE _____

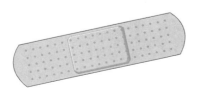

AmE _____

BrE _____

AmE _____

BrE _____

AmE _____

BrE _____

AmE _____   AmE _____   AmE _____

BrE _____   BrE _____   BrE _____

AmE _____   AmE _____   AmE _____

BrE _____   BrE _____   BrE _____

AmE _____   AmE _____   AmE _____

BrE _____   BrE _____   BrE _____

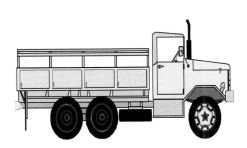
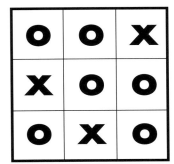
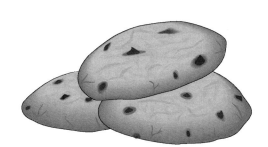

AmE _____   AmE _____   AmE _____

BrE _____   BrE _____   BrE _____

CONFUSABLE NOUNS

The following nouns are often confused. Write the correct word in the sentences below.

| woman – wife | prize – price | game – match | happiness – luck |
| business – shop | husband – man | watch – clock | fault – mistake |

1. My _____ is a very good solicitor. She's the only _____ in her office.
2. There are far too many spelling _____ in your essay.
3. Good _____ with your maths test!
4. We didn't buy that car. The _____ was too high.
5. The football _____ yesterday was very exciting, don't you think?
6. How is _____? Great, I had lots of customers in the _____ today.
7. She wears a gold _____ on her wrist.
8. Who was that _____ I saw her speaking to? Was it her _____?
9. We tried our _____ at the gambling casino.
10. The law in this country is not the same for men and _____.
11. The second _____ is a trip for two to Florida.
12. Despite all her _____ she's a nice and good-natured girl.
13. Excuse me, please, is this the _____'s department? I'm looking for a tie.
14. It's not my _____; after all, it was you who made the _____.
15. My wife's _____ is my only concern at the moment.
16. The _____ tower of the Houses of Parliament in London is often called Big Ben.
17. Has the _____ of eggs gone up again?
18. In an English town there are always many _____ in the High Street.
19. I wish you and your wife every _____ in your married life!
20. Outdoor _____ are high on the agenda at public schools in England.

CONFUSING NOUNS

The words in italics below regularly cause problems because they have similar, but not identical, meanings. Choose the correct word in each of the following sentences and then use the empty line to write your own sentence containing the alternative word to show you've understood the difference in meanings.

1. My daughter has got a summer *work / job* as a guide at the Tower of London.

2. Turn right into Victoria Road and the second *building / house* on your left is the library.

3. Amsterdam is a city famous for its *channels / canals*.

4. I'd love to bake a German cake for your birthday but I can't find the *receipt / recipe*.

5. Mrs Tyler wrote the message on the *backside / back* of the envelope.

6. New York is one of the largest *towns / cities* in the United States.

7. A *suite / suit* is a set of clothes of matching material for men, usually consisting of a jacket and trousers.

8. She heard the *noise / sound* of footsteps on the landing and felt very frightened.

9. He smokes five *packages / packets* of cigarettes a day.

10. I'm no longer in the *custom / habit* of getting up as early as that!

11. The cost of *life / living* in Britain has risen enormously since the beginning of the 80's.

12. There wasn't enough *space / room* for everybody to move freely.

13. My girlfriend had left a *notice / note* on the kitchen table saying that she would be late getting home.

14. She never did any *housework / homework* and so ended up with very bad marks in school.

Be as good as your word

Choose the correct word to complete these sentences.

1. Have you _____ your homework?   ○ made   ○ committed   ○ done
2. It's difficult for me to find a _____ flat.   ○ passable   ○ suitable   ○ passing
3. My son works _____ at McDonalds.   ○ half-time   ○ spare time   ○ part-time
4. My tolerance has reached its _____ .   ○ boundaries   ○ borders   ○ limits
5. He is a carpenter by _____ .   ○ profession   ○ occupation   ○ trade
6. This newspaper always has catchy _____ .   ○ headlines   ○ overheads   ○ headroom
7. She _____ up the documents in the safe.   ○ closed   ○ shut   ○ locked
8. The _____ in western England is beautiful.   ○ nature   ○ scenery   ○ land
9. All passengers _____ the crash.   ○ surpassed   ○ surveyed   ○ survived
10. Let's have a _____ for lunch!   ○ pause   ○ interval   ○ break
11. I like my men tall, _____ and rich!   ○ pretty   ○ handsome   ○ lovely
12. Anne is very _____ her sister.   ○ likely   ○ like   ○ alike
13. The bus leaves from the _____ nearest the school.   ○ halt   ○ station   ○ stop
14. Brian was very _____ so he went to bed early.   ○ asleep   ○ sleeping   ○ sleepy
15. He often goes on business _____ to France.   ○ journeys   ○ voyages   ○ trips
16. I can _____ you I was there!   ○ insure   ○ ensure   ○ assure

THE GOLDEN MIDDLE

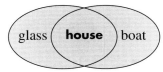

*L*ike *house* in *glasshouse* and *houseboat,* many words can act as both the first and the second half of a compound. Choose from such words in the grey box and combine them with the words in each line. Explain the meaning of each new word and what they have in common, then use them in a sentence.

bank	bed	boy	code	day	field	fish	**house**
light	market	master	school	shirt	shop	wave	work

glass _____ **house** _____ boat

sand _____ note

spot _____ house

language _____ friend

oil _____ mouse

paper _____ force

post _____ word

super _____ place

sweat _____ sleeve

head _____ piece

book _____ keeper

heat _____ length

flower _____ room

pay _____ dream

school _____ friend

gold _____ monger

57

PROFESSIONAL COMPOUNDS

Pair up the words that belong together to get compounds expressing jobs and occupations.

1	tour	**guide**	programmer
2	airline		driver
3	ballet		warden
4	car		star
5	computer		editor
6	construction		farmer
7	customs		teacher
8	newspaper		guard
9	film		pilot
10	traffic		officer
11	football		designer
12	hair		**guide**
13	maths		scientist
14	fashion		dancer
15	research		stylist
16	security		worker
17	sheep		mechanic
18	taxi		player

58

WHEN *ALL* IS SAID AND DONE

In all	**in total number**	you may have it
At all	_____	in summary
For all	_____	nevertheless
All for	_____	in all respects
All over	_____	in spite of
All along	_____	suddenly
All round	_____	everywhere
All yours	_____	**in total number**
All the time	_____	in favour of
All the same	_____	finished
All of a sudden	_____	in any way
All in all	_____	from the start
All over the place	_____	continually

'All right?'
'Yes, thanks.'
'Coming to the club for lunch?'
'All right, see you in half an hour.'

Look at the words and expressions above. They all have something to do with all. Pair them up first and then use them to complete the sentences on this page.

1. He said _____ that we couldn't afford it.
2. If you need any help _____ , please don't hesitate to contact me.
3. I'm _____ anything that makes life easier!
4. _____ her money she's not a happy woman.
5. The wedding was _____ when we arrived at the church.
6. May I borrow your magazine when you've finished with it? There you are, it's _____ .
7. She knew he wasn't listening but she continued _____ !
8. _____ there was a tremendous crash.
9. When we were in Cornwall it rained _____ .
10. In Jim's room there were shoes and clothes _____ .
11. _____ there were seventeen cars lined up in the car park.
12. _____ we had a good day despite the delay at the ferry terminal.
13. A very good performance _____ don't you think?

A Bunch of QUANTITIES

a loaf .... of chocolate
a bar .... of shoes
a roll .... of wine
a packet .... of flowers
a bunch .... of cat food
a bottle .... of bread
a carton .... of honey
a pair .... of milk
a jar .... of toilet paper
a tin .... of cigarettes

Mr and Mrs Branescatter's shopping list is in a bit of a mess; help them to put it right.

a _____ of _____   a _____   a _____
a _____   of _____   of _____
of _____

a _____   a _____   a _____   a _____   a _____   a _____
of _____ of _____ of _____ of _____ of _____ of _____

Partitives are nouns which help to express quantities or amounts of something. Use the partitives from the grey box to complete the sentences.

| bowl |
| breath |
| clap |
| drop |
| flash |
| glass |
| gust |
| lock |
| lump |
| puff |
| sheet |
| slice |
| speck |
| spell |
| stretch |
| sum |
| wink |

1. I'm terribly tired; I didn't get a _____ of sleep last night.
2. The teacher gave each pupil a fresh _____ of paper for the test.
3. Just one _____ of sugar for me, thank you.
4. A sudden _____ of wind blew off Mrs Robinson's hat.
5. He felt a _____ of rain on his hand and decided to go inside.
6. In the army you may get punished for the smallest _____ of dust on your rifle.
7. We've had a marvellous _____ of warm weather recently.
8. It's quite hot in here, I'll just go outside for a _____ of fresh air.
9. A bright _____ of lightning was followed by a loud _____ of thunder.
10. There have already been five accidents on that new _____ of motorway.
11. You shouldn't keep such a large _____ of money at home.
12. Would you like another _____ of cake?
13. A small _____ of smoke came from the professor's pipe.
14. A _____ of hair fell over her forehead and covered her eyes.
15. As Sue is on a diet, she'll just have a _____ of water and a _____ of soup.

60

SCRABBLE

Form as many words as possible with the letters below. Write down the sum of the value points of the letters you used. You can use each letter only once with each word. If you can use all the letters to form a word you get a bonus of 20 points.

U₂ **R**₁ **T**₁ **G**₃ **N**₁ **M**₂ **E**₁ **A**₁

Words	Points	Words	Points	Words	Points	Words	Points
						TOTAL Points:	

A₁ **C**₂ **I**₁ **S**₁ **T**₁ **D**₂ **E**₁ **N**₁

Words	Points	Words	Points	Words	Points	Words	Points
						TOTAL Points:	

R₂ **G**₃ **E**₁ **T**₁ **R**₂ **S**₁ **A**₁ **N**₁

Words	Points	Words	Points	Words	Points	Words	Points
						TOTAL Points:	

FIXED PHRASES — Odd one out

| False | ○ alarm | ✘ book | ○ move | ○ start |

Each of the lines contains three idiomatic fixed phrases and one unacceptable combination. Mark (✘) the odd one out, but also explain the meaning of each fixed phrase and write down their translations in your own language.

1. **First**   ○ aid   ○ class   ○ language   ○ minister
   Translation ▶
2. **Double**   ○ agent   ○ chin   ○ milk   ○ standard
   ▶
3. **Fast**   ○ food   ○ track   ○ boat   ○ breeder
   ▶
4. **General**   ○ knowledge   ○ election   ○ strike   ○ building
   ▶
5. **Free**   ○ enterprise   ○ kick   ○ will   ○ air
   ▶
6. **Green**   ○ ocean   ○ salad   ○ belt   ○ party
   ▶
7. **Foreign**   ○ sun   ○ language   ○ policy   ○ body
   ▶
8. **Personal**   ○ assistant   ○ dog   ○ computer   ○ touch
   ▶
9. **Golden**   ○ handshake   ○ darling   ○ age   ○ rule
   ▶
10. **Hot**   ○ line   ○ dog   ○ air   ○ heating
    ▶
11. **Human**   ○ rights   ○ country   ○ being   ○ nature
    ▶
12. **National**   ○ money   ○ service   ○ park   ○ anthem
    ▶
13. **Open**   ○ secret   ○ question   ○ letter   ○ mouth
    ▶
14. **Private**   ○ detective   ○ property   ○ school   ○ tree
    ▶
15. **Public**   ○ convenience   ○ school   ○ taxes   ○ relations
    ▶

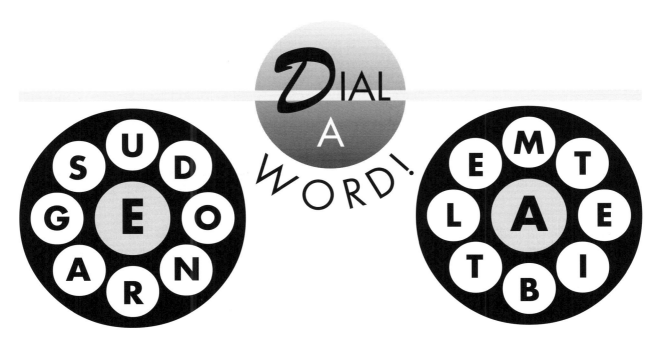

Form words with the letters of the dial. Use each letter as many times as you wish, but the words must contain the letter shown in the middle of the dial. You get more points for longer words.
3 Letters = 1 Point; 4 Letters = 2 Points; 5 Letters = 3 Points; 6 Letters = 4 Points; More = 5 Points; All: 12 Points

3 Letters

4 Letters

5 Letters

6 Letters

More

All Letters

SCORE

3 Letters

4 Letters

5 Letters

6 Letters

More

All Letters

SCORE

63